People
Once Real

Richard Hoffman

LILY POETRY REVIEW BOOKS

Additional praise for Richard Hoffman's poetry:

"If Anton Chekhov returned as a modern-day poet, Richard Hoffman would be his name. His poems reverberate with the same lucid witness and precision. Bridging histories local and cultural, they draw on literary traditions while simultaneously heralding experiment and invention."

> — **Terrance Hayes,** author of *American Sonnets for My Past and Future Assassin*

"Richard Hoffman is a fiercely gifted poet whose stanzas revel in the infinite possibilities of language, and jolt, surprise, and satisfy at every turn. This is work to be savored and embraced."

> — **Patricia Smith,** author of *Incendiary Art*

"Hoffman taps into moments when civilization dissolves, not superficially, but at its emotional roots. Time and again through the poet's weary irony comes the bite of life."

> — **Molly Peacock,** author of *Flower Diary*

"Beautiful and dangerous, unforgettable, transformational, meaningful across academic and social borders."

> — **Linda McCarriston,** author of *Eva-Mary*

"Hoffman is a rarity; his premise is dialogic, his canvas vast, his stance self-questioning. This new book is breakthrough work of hard-earned grounding, profound integrity, and scalding, visionary intensity."

> — **D. Nurkse,** author of *A Country of Strangers: New & Selected Poems*

"Hoffman is the poet traveling our nightmare of now, our descent into a lack of love for one another, but along the way he finds etchings of hope on the walls amid all the signs of a falling away from a center that has forgotten how to hold. Hoffman's tropes and incantations invite us to shed a wisdom that has grown archaic so that we can begin to reclaim the genuine and live."

— **Afaa Michael Weaver**

for Kathi

A Letter to Walt Whitman in the Earth

Walt, under my boot-soles
you smell like naphthalene and paint
whenever the water table rises, and no one
is held accountable. You were irascible
post-stroke, talked bigotry
that marred the glory of your work,
a mite infected eagle come to earth,
clumsy, ripping the neighborhood garbage bags.
But I need your *Homo sum*..., your orchestral acapella,
singing of us already in my great grandfather's time.
Now generalists with cell phones selling wellness
on the beltways of America at eighty mph believe
they are the first to want a life that's more than labor
and have made that aim a creed. They pray: May I get mine.
Your beautiful roughs are trained to kill,
contractors now, not camerados,
and none are heard above the mating calls
of money sounding in the air instead of the flocks
of sparrows you heard in Camden. Do I sound bitter?
Very well then, I am bitter. I am large. I contain
our entire betrayal, Walt — caged children, murdered
citizens, poisoned water, spent uranium — by those
for whom democracy's an obstacle and humans
resources. And it's hard to feel amative, loafing here,
my soul so far declining my invitation, maybe
because a surveillance cam has noted me, a kosmos,
and is now uploading my worried face and stats
to a gleaming satellite in orbit high above These States.

TABLE OF CONTENTS

Mundus et Infans

1. Mundus

Horizon: November 14, 2016

A giant copper moon flares on the lake
in the early dark, and on the car radio, talk.
Talk trying to chew despair. Talk about fear
to hide fear. Talk about talk about talk.
Fifty cents, a dollar a word. It is all just talk

until it isn't. A day may come soon
when we pay with our lives for the lives
of our friends. What else did we ever have
to pay with? What else were we ever for?
Each ripple on the lake is a lick of flame.

Betrayal

One's-self I sing, a simple separate person
                                    — Whitman

Earth's tragicomic bricolage,
        I am imagined

of necessity and desire — oh,
and fear; mustn't forget fear.

So I see angels
jutting from corbels and cornices,
their appearance

            suggested by air conditioners
            high above the avenues

        as the planet
reaches combustion temperature
        and a bit of friction here or there
            burns down a city

of people reading, playing, cooking, sleeping,
sharing their innocent puzzlement,

telling one another their neighborly lies.

            Shrieking mirror
        neurons split the atoms
belonging to me, belonging to you, and

corruption runs in the gutters
        and celebrates itself,
laughing and only mildly ashamed.

Now everyone can see the future
      as if possessed
of powers they never had before,
         though most refuse.

My country, 'tis
      a giant clock
above a loud arena of applauding victims,
      and children without the choice
         not to believe.

D(r)one

What was done was done
in our names; we ourselves

would never have done
what was done to anyone.

We wanted to be good,
polite, obedient, fun,

wanted only not to need
to ask *What have we done?*

And yet, in our names,
what was done was done.

Penitentiary

One day
people will come to tour this place —

walls within walls,
bright slinkies of razor wire,

lighthouse corners, sentries,
(an inverted fortress,
search-lights sweeping inward,)

enmity injurious beyond
calculus, down generations,

— school buses will wait in a row
while children are taught about laws
by then archaic or else

Wurst Haus

In the dream, Brecht and Rilke are having lunch and I'm their waiter. I recognize them — Rilke's doe eyes and moustache, Brecht's balding bowl-cut and glasses. I try not to show my excitement.

I only understand, from hearing it in childhood, a little bit of Deutsch. Brecht keeps trying to turn the conversation to something about an apple tree in blossom but Rilke, panicked and very near tears, is begging Brecht to fill him in on all that happened.

Rilke keeps shaking his head, saying "How is this possible? How could this have happened?"

The old woman in the kitchen putting up the steaming plates of wurst and schnitzel is my German grandmother. I tell her what little I understood.

She wonders, aloud, what in Gott's name these poets are doing in Pennsylvania. Wiping her hands on a towel she goes to the doorway and listens. Soon she rocks back into the kitchen in her heavy shoes, shaking her head. "Goethe!" she says, "Ach! Get out there! Offer them something. Anything. On the house. Don't let them get started on Goethe or we'll never be rid of them!"

As I approach the table, I see that Rilke is weeping. Brecht offers him a handkerchief from his canvas coat. "There, there, little bird," he says, "You needn't worry. This is the future. We're in America now."

Imagine a Future

with no thought to efficiency or deadlines,
and without this fear of the spreading stain

of cozening burlesques supplanting joy,
plastic fool's gold, funny money, blood

on the floorboards scrubbing will never lift
from the grain: where might we begin?

A jury deliberates in every injury,
in each a possibility, an emblem better

than scales and a blindfolded woman,
especially one with a brandished sword.

If you're not a prisoner, you're a guard,
walking the catwalk, weighted with keys.

But let's leave metaphor for another day.
Here we sit facing one another, our knees

touching, hands joined, frightened, learning
what we need, what each of us will need to do.

How To Get By

Since 2015, police officers have fatally shot at least 135 unarmed Black people nationwide. The majority of officers were white, ...

— NPR, Morning Edition, January 5, 2021

Forget what you've seen, and for your own sake,
give up understanding what you've understood.
Call it an accident, not hatred. Call it a mistake.

Pretend you're like the others. Do your best to fake
their manias and worries, carry on as if you could
forget what you've seen, and for your own sake

don't get caught in conversations that may take
your taking a stand. It wasn't, after all, your blood.
Call it an accident, not hatred. Call it a mistake

a good person, fearful and confused, might make,
and don't object when fear is based on falsehood.
Forget what you've seen, and for your own sake,

no matter what you're thinking, be opaque.
Let others project on you what suits their mood.
Call it an accident, not hatred. Call it a mistake

to think your outrage, your anger, your heartache,
if spoken, might change anything or do any good.
Forget what you've seen, and for your own sake,
call it an accident, not hatred. Call it a mistake.

Refrigerator

Old white conserv-
ative, it grumbles,

shudders in its sleep,
and dreams of snow, of
white bears shaking
themselves dry and
rolling on their backs.

When move it must,
it resembles a giant
penguin.

Soft avocadoes,
rubbery artichokes,
bad meat, black bananas,
milk gone sour,
and waxen cheese,

are not its fault.
We are to blame,

our capricious hungers.

Black Friday

They're having another buy one get
the other shoe free sale and the people
borrow at interest so as not to miss it.
The Fire Dept. hired a new arsonist.
This year's boats sport perforated hulls,
and there's a party over on the island
to which, of course, you are not invited.

Still dressing for yesterday's weather
and calling your weaknesses virtues,
you, deep in the fear of being left out,
are already so far out nobody hears you.
For your penance say five your mamas
and five hail hail the gang's all here.
Whatever. Just do the shrug and shuffle.

An ego ago you were king, now nothing
you do or say amounts to anything any-
body gives a fart for. What is art for?
you keep asking as if there is an answer.
You want things on the up and up when
over and over we're going down, down.
We're going to get to the bottom of this.

Why Not Is The New Normal

I passed the things I passed too fast.
Now I walk slowly, listening,
as if for a voice,
to the gravel crunch beneath my shoes.

No future was anyone's friend for long.
With whatever's left let's see what's what.

Contrast

What if this moment is the opposite
of the change to color in Wizard of Oz? —
B&W now making things explicit,

requiring us to choose, to commit.
What if there is no escape because
this is that moment? Is the opposite

of dazzling color clarifying spirit?
Can we address our many traumas?
B&W now making things explicit,

we see the old footage, counterfeit
and colorized, and grasp what it does.
What if this moment is the opposite

of cant and evasion and bullshit,
of any and all the pastel nostalgias,
B&W now making things explicit

so we're finally freed from our habit
of dressing abuse in colorful disguises?
What if this moment is the opposite,
B&W now making things explicit?

The Hole

There's a hole in this poem, a hole
where all the usual ways I know
to write a poem are stuffed to block
the cold wind of the unexpected,

a hole that allows the loud world
to decide which portion of itself
to poke through and require me
to describe it or address it, a hole

that, left open, keens and moans,
howls or bellows as what blows
through it sounds like a sorrow
that would be mine if I so chose.

But not tonight. Tonight I seal
and caulk the breach with what
my words can also do: protect me
until morning when I'm stronger.

Shelter

Mercury and Regulus below bright Venus
rise an hour before the dawn when no one,
or few, are awake to see them fade: brief
harbingers of what? Another hurricane?
An earthquake like the one that rocked
Oaxaca yesterday? Or wildfires as in
Oregon or California? The wind means
to tell us something. Try as we might
to deny it, there is vengeance in the rain
like a barrage of bullets. There is danger
and rage and yes, malice, in the flames,
arson or not, reason aside; adrenaline
is suddenly sufficient metaphysics.
Maybe the wind's eliding vowels mean
nothing, but not to us. Tonight, the moon
and Uranus in Pisces, Delta Cephei is
pulsing an unbroken code, and the sky
is battened over us, a drum. Ions charge
the air: bones know a storm will come.

Vaccine

What is the word for the way
the starling's sheen and the carapace
of the Japanese beetle seem alike?
And if I find it will the dying stop?

Words don't come easily to me.
I used to think they were afraid of me,
they hid in my chest, in my belly.
Will the right ones make the dying stop?

What word is there for the way
some words unsaid erase you?
For our hope not to hurt again?
For what to say to make the dying stop?

Tenebrae

Today I'm a wisp of smoke from cold ashes,
and I don't see a Phoenix egg. Do you?

A broken vase of red carnations, meat on the floor,
a future of slivers and shards and splintered bone.

Everything my father feared, all that my mother
knew but could not say: *Pulvis et umbra sumus,*

use and meaning the same, no use to know good,
some tide pulling love away, exposing the words

meant to hold together several generations to see
further, where only experience discerns what time

has been up to, or at least comes to believe it can,
is all rubble for hungry scavengers, scrap to be sold.

I am, as always, a little bit out of it, but come on,
honestly, wasn't the light there sometimes beautiful?

Caravaggio's torchlight trembling on dark armor,
as Christ is taken post-betrayal? The other martyrs

to impossible belief might be said to have known
something, no? Tell me they did, that it isn't all

a kind of gyascutus, one leg shorter than the other,
grazing the steep green hillside of our needy credulity,

propped up by this or that one's mercantile words,
dark portrait of a forbear who appears to emerge

from the somber past, frowning and cautioning,
but is really only covered in accumulated grime.

Last Hope

If you ever come, my dreamed of world,
the one we almost had, I will be gone
with all the others. After all this waiting
on wooden benches outside in the hall,
after the clicking of heels on polished tile,
after the furious shuffling of papers
and the endless arguments over money,
bring with you people refreshed by love,
disposed to wonder, surprised at cruelty.
Improbable world I once believed in, rising
from words like steam from a bowl of soup,
world like an egg in a nest of the best debris,
if against all odds you take shape one day,
bring people whose hearts are less hesitant,
new people, better people than we were.

They That Mourn

Blessed are they that remember,
for them the muscle of the heart
is twisted as if it is turning away,

or trying to, and what it turns from
is both particle and wave, emitted
from past disaster
but illuminating nothing;

theirs is more than remains.

And blessed are they
that mourn the animals,
that weep for the burning trees,

that roar at the roaring flames
and worry few tears before
were real as these, that turn

the light out, let the night in
and contend with sorrow,

that imagine
what once they are gone
they might wish they had done

and, in that darkness, begin.

Raptor

A silhouette, mostly, in clear October sky.
A goshawk maybe, or a broad-winged,
I'd have to see it again; I can only tell you
I heard its cry and felt its gaze, a laser,
before I passed beneath the aging trees
and kept on, walking and thinking all day.
At dusk the lamps along the path came on,
and lit the leaves a bright unnatural color.
I never knew trees that seemed to worry
so much about what they might say to me
as those along the paved walk out of there:
To be truthful is to remember and grieve.
Then headlights, tail lights, highway, night,
a few clouds passing a half moon, stars.

Kyrie

10/31/2020

Samhain, and a Blue Moon's near red Mars.
The days grow shorter and more hard hours
      are added to our nights.
The angel of history feels useless; she told me
in a nightmare filled with the pornography
      of sadness and its delights.
Sing kyrie, sing kyrie eleison;
none of us should suffer this darkness alone.

Foundlings on earth, from hell or heaven,
at night our shadows show us what will happen,
      and in the morning, rising,
we become again their vital obstruction.
Who abandoned us is a useless question
      unworthy of all the arguing.
Sing kyrie, sing kyrie eleison:
May all earth's deadly resentments be done.

The wind picks up and whistles in the woods.
Days pass fast as breaks in hastened clouds.
      The angel of history shrugs
and throws up her hands, "I told you so!"
but what it was she told we'll never know;
      she speaks in tongues.
Sing kyrie, sing kyrie eleison:
Restore our terrifying human minds to reason.

Live Coverage

I would like beamed to me from the Muse's tower high atop Parnassus
        through one of those earpieces
with the squiggly wire you hide behind your head when in front of the camera
            a few clear words to choose from

for what I have seen, for what is right in front of me and for what perhaps
        is coming soon after that because
though others living through other times were able to imagine a future,
            I, for one, cannot, so just a glimpse

of the day after tomorrow please, just a sense of consequence to rely on
        is all I ask: is this thing on?
I'm not really looking for some kind of woo-woo dictation from the divine;
            I am not so pretentious as that but

what poet in his right mind would not be envious of that stained glass evangel
        who stares up at the angel
held there in the air by wings and holding an unfurled scroll of cryptic text
            that, translated, tells what's next

simply by pointing out what happens over and over again unceasingly but
        hidden by the surrounding minutiae
that make up our creaturely, phlegmatic, obligated and dutiful daily lives
            we ought to count as mercy

for their blurring and obscuring most of the time precisely that prophetic
        clarity the angel is offering,
flying in place like a hummingbird but ready to dart away any moment
            so fast you wonder if you saw it.

I need a few suggestions just to get me started how to talk about the way
        not a blessed thing I believed,
not a single axiom holds anymore, like the guy on the Weather Channel
            out in the middle of the storm,

waves crashing on the seawall, wind roaring and popping in his microphone,
    with one hand cupping his ear,
words blown away or drowned out by thunder and the roar of the sea,
    camera lens streaked by tears.

2. Infans

Late Elegy

Too young to know better,
my brother and I ate flowers,
pink rose petals; their veins,
I think, convinced us we could,
the thin capillaries in the flesh
of roses heavy on our family's
wicker trellis or hanging over
the neighbors' rickety fence.
We smuggled salt from the kitchen,
sat in the grass, feasted, laughed.
The part of me that might have
remembered what we said was
not yet alive. I only know we
wanted so much to be good
we must have believed we weren't.
One petal at a time, a little salt.
My brother and I ate flowers.

i.m. RJH

Unearthed

Digging, I struck a small box
and lifted it from the earth.

Inside, coiled, a golden wire,
like a single bronze piano wire.

Freed, it sprung and lashed me,
almost putting out my eye.

I took it home and stretched it
from the lintel to the threshold

and strummed it. Don't ask me
how I knew it was my brother.

It made a sound I remembered.
Not his mutinous broken body

but some other part of him,
perhaps the sound for him I made

when our mother first lay him
beside me in our crib, my name

for him before I knew his name.
Now, decades beyond a time

his given name can call him,
I am here with my yearning,

in the doorway, tuning myself,
thrumming his one bass note.

Bobber

The two tall boys, brothers, both
with wire-rimmed glasses, with wicker
creels, fly-fishing gear, and vests
with patches of sheepskin shearling
dotted with trout flies, worked their way
downstream in their rubber waders.
When they passed where I sat,
watching my red and white bobber
under a tree limb decorated with
colorful lures, hooks, shiny spoons,
and dangling tangled fishing line,
I felt shame. They might have been
aristocrats, those tall twins. "Hey,"
I waved. "You catching anything?"
They looked at each other, smiled,
and sloshed downstream to the bend.
Or maybe they were a year apart like
my younger brother Bobby and me.
People said we looked like twins.
Once we brought Bobby to fish
from his wheelchair. He caught nothing
and didn't much enjoy himself;
I could tell from the look he gave me,
and from the look he gave me after that
whenever I left the house with my rod.
I envied those fortunate boys their
fancy tackle as I sat there, alone,
with my coffee can of nightcrawlers,
staring at my plastic bobber, wanting
to hurt one or the other of them badly,
and plotting to leave that place forever.

Trapdoor

Grief is the floor.
        There is a door there,

                a door in the floor:

        on the other side,
                on the underside, in the dark,

        along with pipes and wires, is what
                rests
        on what, what now
                        and again shifts,
                settles,
        shears.

I miss my brothers.

Dialogue

I went to a nearby cemetery
        to speak with some other dead

because the dead are all the same
        and laugh that same bitter laughter,

as if my need to understand
        why I am alive and my brothers dead

is foolish anywhere, and even though
        they know they will not tell me.

In Memoriam

Shadows, they remain
inside the outline of my shadow always
          as per our agreement,
     their abiding cool desire,
               and the laws of light.
I have sometimes stayed with them
     all night in the dark
when we can be most ourselves
          together.

If they had a word
     for when the sun rises
it would be the same as our word
          for remembering,
and because we are never really apart
               we call it mine,
     this time since their deaths,

as if time must belong to someone,
          as if I were not a shadow too,
     as if we were not all
               the sun's
misshapen children.

Addict

As a child I saw

faces convulse in disbelief
              and silent mourners
at graveside in black coats quake
        under bowed heads

and couldn't help wanting
            to console us all
      but couldn't

I was only a child
          so I made myself

sick, over and over,
        to have an excuse if ever
          I was asked

if I could remember
         what I thought
      love had charged me to do.

Benedictus

She took the amber rosary
        from his hands in the casket
draped it on the vanity's mirror
        (the crowded smoky living
room empty at last of pity)
        but she can't believe now
or every morning left her
        she would have to pray:
You give me skies and trees
        and rivers and days and months
and years in return for my child
        and his laughter and all we knew
together and all we never got to do
        together and think it's enough?
She savors her bitter black
        coffee, her only breakfast,
sun coming over the houses,
        day's first long shadows.

How I Burned

Like a candle: as the robed boy receded, I streamed a wavering and fragrant smoke.

Like a log: I wept when I recalled the tree, tears wrung from me, hissing in blue flame; when I recalled the forest, I crackled and sparked and wanted to escape, to roll from my place and onto your carpet, burn down your house.

Like a fuse: I thought I was a seed. I thought what I'd been given was a life. I learned to call the sound I made a meaning, and that meaning would be evident and glorious one day. I called that faith.

Like a house: my picture in the news, I was furious to become a figure of speech. Now you can't come back, ever.

Like a comet: I hoped to arrive somewhere while there was something left of me besides the memory of a streak across a night sky nearly everyone ignores and few can read and understand.

Like a heretic: even before the flames caught my clothes, the heat had emptied my words and shown me my enemy's were also hollow. I could have spoken, my tongue was not yet burned, but I had lost my faith — not only in my words but anyone's.

Like a pile of rags: in the aftermath of every purpose, I remained for awhile of some use. Designed to hold, shape, disguise, protect, hide, cleanse, it didn't take much: the bodies I had touched made me combustible.

Like a torch: (but some were foolish and took no thought for the length of the night, no measure of the tunnel, and were left in darkness.)

Like a pilot light: My virtue was humility. Hidden, I dreamed of a great conflagration.

Like a bonfire: of driftwood and broken branches, my purpose was to gather the people around me. Their purpose I left to them.

Like a book: By the time they burned me it was already too late. By the time they got home, their houses were in flames.

Autobiography

The fish I caught
I called rainbows.
I was wrong.

They were promises.
I call them memories
now, downstream.

I am not fooling.
I have brought it all.
Nothing is lost.

That broken boy,
suddenly brotherless,
alone by the brook,

I have tried
to make him a life
to look forward to.

Album

They turn to me, my parents, as if they see me,
as if they might respond, but go on dancing.

For how many years they went on dancing,
shoes resoled and resoled, long out of fashion,

she with her net veil, crisp and scratchy,
attached to a hat of satin roses, in a crinkly dress

that wraps her like a package, he in his heavy
herringbone, brown, with baggy knees. Young,

filled with necessities and niceties and faith,
they wonder at me: *what are you staring at?*

Mt. Moriah

A black ant struggled to lug
a crumb a robin dropped
from bread my mother
scattered from the door;
a bee palpated clover blossoms,
somehow like my mother
choosing peaches, or rooting
in the drawer of her vanity
for something discarded.
When I took my father's hand
to switchback up the mountain
of oaths and cutthroat promises
what did we lose? We labored
up the littered, designated trail,
our progress equal to the sum
of all he taught me to ignore.
My father stopped, sighed,
reached down deep in his bag.
"Let's get this over with," he said,
aloud, to no one I could see.

Formica

I'm eleven. My father hears me say "fuck"
and decides it's time for the talk.
It's my mother's kitchen but she's not there.

I believe he was a little drunk, just loose
not sloppy. He began, several times,
starting over, pulling on a tall brown bottle,

saying my skinny body would pretty
soon change. I watched from far behind
my thank you daddy good boy mask

as he said that men and women fit together
and yes he used his finger and made the O
like OK, sliding in and out. The man's organ,

he used the word *organ*, becomes inflamed,
he used the word *inflamed*, until it spits a
seed inside the woman and that's how babies

come. Do you have any questions son?
He said that it was beautiful, really, as if
he knew he'd failed to make it seem that way.

He said that it was holy. He didn't know
my coach with his crooked *organ* had already
inflamed my pretty body, burning me to ash.

And there and then in that kitchen I froze
what was left of the two of us like cut bait.
Decades gurgled in the pipes below the sink.

The clouds in the tabletop purled like smoke.
On the wall sad Jesus pointed to his heart.
The calendar offered a dozen scenic elsewheres.

That Water

A clear brook, spring-fed, gurgled over rocks
deep in a forest where my parents brought me
one hot summer as a boy. Now both of them
are dead, so I can't ask them where to find it,
but I will never forget how that water tasted.
If you take a metal spoon, freeze water in it,
then thaw it again and as soon as it is liquid
touch your tongue to it, you'd have an idea.
Or fresh rainwater, maybe, from a pie-tin,
but rainwater is not as cold, and could not
wake you like that, so for a moment you hear
insects scrabbling on pebbles, mossy stones
humming greenly to themselves, and the light
applauding. That water will never let you go.

Hurricane

An old gray oak
downed in the street.
I was five. Fallen
on its side, impossible

roots above me.
In the street, a wire
twitched and sparked.

Then I was lifted
on my father's shoulders.

Dusk

I will die in Paris in a rainstorm,
on a day I already remember.
                    —*Cesar Vallejo*
                    (tr. Andres Rojas)

Whether or not there is a river,
I will be by a river. My mother
will send my father to fetch me.
He will toot the horn twice and I
will wish for more time. As usual,
I've caught nothing. And whether
or not I have already given up,
I will know I have to go. I will
put my gear in the trunk. Whump.
He will lean across the front seat
and swing open the door, and I
will enter the musk of the car,
the smoky sweat of my father,
and note the regret on his face.
Though I was not always glad
to see him, I am glad to see him.
Whether or not I want more time,
the sky will continue darkening.
Already there are stars, and waist
high at the wood's edge, fireflies.
My father clutches and shifts,
then touches me on the shoulder,
staring ahead, eyes on the road.

A Reflection

Some days I wake feeling drugged,
incoherent, the sunrise itself
an intrusion, others I'm raw and sad

and each new thing, each person,
even every new thought, feels too late:
How could I not have noticed this? Why

did I never think of that before? How
have I met this striking person only now?
And only the familiar has no sorrow.

These are the days, I know by now,
my dead surround me; I sense them
when the beam of my sad attention

is reflected back at me the way
the eyes of animals shine back at night,
the only evidence they're there.

A Church

I heard music so I went inside.

Just below the altar, behind the rail
        with its open gate,
a chamber orchestra played Vivaldi.

I found a place, alone, not too far back,
behind the others scattered here and there.

The music was sublime, and

if not for the hanging lamps,
        the stained glass windows,
the statues and carved figures,
        the decorated corbelled arches,

I might have closed my eyes,

but everything called my gaze
upward, even as Vivaldi carried on
enthusiastically about *La Primavera*

and there, above the sanctuary
high in the painted dome,
between a symbol I knew and one I didn't,

a branching crack

and for the whole remainder of Spring

I wondered, for the life of me,
how anyone could ever get up there to fix it.

A Prayer For The Souls In Purgatory

I return from the future,
a spy, and imagine myself

the old woman in the lawn chair
in front of the apartment house on the corner, nylons rolled
to her ankles, smoking a cigarette, watching.

     And then for a moment I'm the aproned grocer
picking over his produce in front of the store,
hand-cranking down the screeching awning to keep
the hot sun off the cantaloupe,
retrieving his short pencil from among the oranges
and replacing it behind his ear.

          After that I might become
the cabbie at the taxi stand, in mirrored sunglasses,
his elbow sticking out the window,
listening to WAEB.

     Or the letter carrier in his eight pointed cap,
with his pockets full of dog biscuits.

Because someone must have seen something.

     I'll turn myself into Sister Maria Elena,
the sixth grade class before me.

        Or I'll make myself
one or the other of the white-haired couple
          rocking on their front porch
as the children pass on their way from school.

I am looking for what the boy did
just after what was done to him,

when the cairn of his years toppled,
when the stream of his days was diverted,

                    but neither that place nor
any of those people remain. Neither do I
remember to whom I meant to report all this.

2.

Someone must have heard something

over the pipe organ wobbling the cupped candles,
shivering the skin on the holy water in the doorway fonts,

over Top 40 on transistors, above the deafening
Harleys down Main, or the sirens of the air-raid drills,

(war memories refreshed, relief repurposed,
march-of-progress rhetoric, plenty for sale.)

If he had cried out, that boy,
would anyone have heard?

He made certain no one would
by never crying, ever.

3.

Old now, I continue
        to turn from oblivion
                for as long as I can, so long

as there are births and birdsong,
    libraries to fathom,
        tempos that change.

                            I forgive

        their inattention: not one of them
    from whom I would
withhold untroubled dying.

O

There is a moment of such pain,
beside an open grave,
when someone must hold you up,

when the only difference that matters
is between the living and the dead:

　　　Could we remember, O,
　　　what hatred could survive?

Solitude

This morning I am that pearly koi,
     shape and weight
     of a buoyed heart,
         a scarlet cauliflower on my head,
flanks contoured like a horse's jaw,
     my tail a billowing silk: you,
tapping the glass,

what do you want from me?

I Don't Recall Where We Were Going

When we set out, the downpour
was so loud I didn't hear you ask
if we should pull over. I'm sorry.
The child in the backseat followed
a rivulet's path down the window
as if instructive, and the wipers,
struggling to keep up, said life is
luck and love and love and luck and
luck and love as I tried to stay on
the road, torrents pouring across it,
great fans of water slapping us
from gigantic trucks roaring past.
I dared not turn and look at you.
I never was so frightened or alive

.

A Love Song

You were water rinsing crusted blood
from the stone altar where a chieftain
held a young boy's heart up to the sun.

I was the man who cried out and knew,
that first day, I would stay with you,
that even my anger never stood a chance.

I knew I loved you, and I said so then.
But how I love you now makes that a lie.

Impenitent Thief

Once a young woman heard
a baby's cry
coming from the house of death;

bloodied and fierce she entered,
snatched the child,
and barely made it out of there,

the two of them alive.

"Dear child, you are mine," she whispered,
rocking the sleeping infant in her arms.

Later, older, hurt by words, the child
would turn and plunge into her
like someone on fire into a pool of water.

"You are my child and I am your mother,"
the woman would sing then, soothing the child.

But she had never forgotten,
no mother has ever forgotten,

from whom she'd stolen it.

The Underworld

Something was blocking the drain.
"I'll have to get a snake in there,"
the plumber said. "We'll have to plumb
the mystery," he added and winked.
No doubt he'd said this many times.

I obliged him with a smile, anxious
for him to get to work. "Trees," he said.
"You got roots all under here, below the floor,"

and the way he gestured then,
with both hands, made me think
about the twisted mulberry and red maples
shading the house but buckling the driveway,

and how much farther than their sheltering
boughs their roots go, knuckled and groping,

so that if earth receded, shrank,
we'd be here, in this house,
in its branches, like a winter nest.

Remorse

The young moon in the west after sunset,
here it is clear and cold and I am lonely.
When I step on a twig I can hear I have
broken something, and all at once you
are here with me, my face wet in my hands.

Dingle

We must have come from the sea
where love's debris moves deep
in darkness. You were with me,
I'm sure, in that current, that lunar

pull we feel, still, in our throats,
a yearning to break and roar,
a gathering desire, desperately
looking for a shore to die on

or begin. Here are hydrangea,
fuchsia, olearia in sea-breeze,
silver underneath, as if clouds
were moving across the sun,

changing everything; then rain,
its salt smell, sideways from the sea.

A Marriage

You whom I love most
were reading beneath a tree,
and as I approached,
birds in twos and threes
arrived and filled the branches
until the tree was loud
with twittering, nervous birds
flitting from branch to branch.
Then a thundering of wings,
like a single cry as they departed.
O my love there is more,
much more, still, to know
of love than how to continue.

Comfort

Hearing the rain on the roof above our bed.
Saying *the roof above.* Saying *our bed.*

A Summer Nap

I dreamed I had died
and didn't tell anybody.

It was my death;
none of their business.

When I met the angels
they were all the same

birds I'd been hearing,
uncomprehending,

all my life. And when
I woke I recalled the way

their singing felt but no
words, not in this world,

though I'm now convinced
there's more joy to be had

than I ever before believed
I might allow myself.

Winter Island Park

Gulls work the shallows mid-tide.
Clouds bear down on the harbor.
Below the seawall, in a dimpled
pool: starfish, sea urchins, snails.

Soon rainwater's weight weighs
down day lilies, irises, and bright
beach roses along the gravel path.
Whenever I come here I become

a kind of pronoun, someone
someone might see standing
on the jetty, or climbing the rocks,
or, today, rain soaked, suddenly

beginning to run, car keys in hand,
his particular life returned to him.

November Suite

1.

At first I held out my hands, then my arms,
to welcome and hold
all that was offered. In time I learned
that none of it could be abandoned.

I learned how to walk slightly bent
and adjust my gait to the terrain and to the pace
of those I love. Having wanted so much,
having accepted so much, now possessing so much,
what could I do but carry it?

2.

A song about a song is a kind of prayer,
and I needed to pray,
but failed for the need to be sure I was heard.

3.

To watch the amber moon rise,
whitening in the darkening sky

requires peace, and even now
a lover to tell you your head

grows heavier drifting into sleep.
Who else might spare you

from becoming someone else
again? Who else offer refuge

now from self-injury? Love
is required, yes, but also fact:

the moon from night to night
changes as if our own vast

shadow, otherwise invisible,
were passing over it like memory,

but that's illusion— our shadow,
though dark and far-reaching,

has nothing to do with it —
and love, I've come to believe,

has little to do with memory,
and what it calls for one has

in the present or not at all,
so I can say only that tonight,

as you quieted, and your breath
slowed, your tired white head,

resting on my shoulder, seemed
heavier and even dearer to me.

4.

And the ragged birds of grief have their work to do as well,
our *misereres* their summons, our indignation,
our tears their signal to gather and wheel,

while down below, where we cannot
and do not wish to see, our beloved is still
not entirely earth, still largely memory.

5.

So now I know memory
has distance in it,

something like pleasure
in seeing the rain
a mile or so away across the harbor
come steadily closer,

or looking up
from under the lamp on the bridge at snow
that appears to come unending from the darkness,
swirling like summer's moths,

then, as it nears,
(and as it nears it comes faster
or seems to)
I resign myself
to breathing the air Gautama
and Stalin, during their brief seasons,
shared with the trees

because now I understand I was unfaithful
to the wordless oath I swore in my mother's womb,
to never not desire to be,

and so ineligible, for all that time, for joy.

6.

Here hibiscus blooms midsummer
and I try to conceive of time
without numbers, as nothing I can hope
to grasp in any language I already understand:
how long has it taken

for the ivy, trembling on this crumbling wall
to have climbed this far? The wind

would tear the leaves from the vine
if they were another shape. And we

require of ourselves and one another
too many things we imagine necessary.

"Fantastic Voyage"

1.

Like one of the characters from that old matinee, I am inside the heart
but somehow it is my own heart and I am inside a humming room, waiting

before a round door I know to be a valve that will admit a flood of the past,
a forceful torrent of what is depleted, the valve like a spaceship's airlock,

and before I open it I must unlock the corresponding valve in the far wall,
which I understand is the future, and stand back, or history will drown me.

2.

There are these griefs, you see, starved, desiccated as the tiny corpses
of insects left in abandoned webs that quiver with my movements

here in this creaky attic or cellar, someplace I don't visit often
enough to recognize the things I have piled there haphazardly.

Anything of worth I find here I find looking for something else
among the things I chose to store away for some other, easier life.

3.

Inside me are places where conclusions and confessions are conjecture
because the dead have left behind them a film of sticky shame

and a granulated record of deeds and misdeeds like the residue of sleep
around the eyes each morning. Merrily, merrily, merrily, merrily I pull

the cord to try to start the engine but my little boat drifts downstream
toward the falls highlighted on the map. Maybe it won't be so bad.

3. Mundus et Infans

Mundus et Infans

The Angel that presided o'er my birth
Said, "Little creature, form'd of Joy and Mirth,
"Go love without the help of any Thing on Earth."
                                                    — *Blake*

1. *After The War*

Waves went on rolling across leagues of water.
Clouds hit high-pressure zones and piled up into new beauties.
A woman who lived alone cracked an egg on the rim of a pan.
A zygote, many zygotes, became
attached, precariously, to nourishing uterine walls.
A petulant dictator on the rise professed his admiration
for a spurious book deemed holy to those he planned to kill.
In regions newly designated countries
by people in countries elsewhere, resentments seethed.
A dozen academic papers sifted evidence
for calling a set of symptoms a new disease.
In the meantime and long before I knew myself at all,
my life had begun among ghosts who begged to be mourned
or demanded answers, especially the ones who didn't know
they had been murdered — wrong name, faith, country.
I lay there, a little red fist, and wailed, but no one saw
that they surrounded me, asking for pity, or vengeance,
or begging forgiveness for crimes against me, maledictions
like unexploded ordnance in the neighborhood.
People once real, who'd loved their lives, and one another,
who might not have meant to harm but only warn me —
in what first tongue did I compose those poems
that calmed them, that bid them be silent so I could sleep?
I need that language now. They have returned. They circle,
insistent, whispering: *same war, same war, same war.*

2. *Art A Great Investment, Says Forbes*

For sale at auction: wooden Santos
     from Mexico
hand-painted in colorful uniforms,
rough-hewn, nearly identical
     figurines,
swords drawn, holding
children's bloody heads, arms, legs,
     arranged
in the Sotheby's brochure around
     a screaming mother:

The Massacre of the Innocents, artist unknown.

A recurrent theme in western art:
Rubens, Breughel, Poisson, Ghirlandaio.

Amid the charred ribs of a school bus
in Yemen, a fragment of fuselage:
Commercial and Government Entity Code
C.A.G.E.
like a return address:

Lockheed Martin/General Dynamics
Burlington, Massachusetts/Falls Church, Virginia

"... engineering a better tomorrow."

And in the bramble a ram entangled:
O angel of outrage, where are you?

for arms say
Aerospace

for surveillance
Information Systems

for bombers say
Defense

for taxes
say Earnings

say 2nd quarter
on track

say 62
billion US dollars

A voice was heard in Ramah.
Rachel weeping for her children.

A Saudi apologist claimed
the Yemeni school was teaching
                insurrection.
King Herod's fear. Precisely Herod's fear.

In Breughel's version, blood
        on the village snow. In Ghirlandaio's, blood
                on the plaza's stones,
imperial architecture in the background.

In Poussin's a sandaled soldier, his foot
        on a baby's neck, dispassionately
                sights down the blade. In the Rubens, it is hard
to separate the mothers from their babies;
        the scene is one great mass of writhing flesh.

At the border, the official explained, it is hard
to separate the mothers

from Mexico

from their babies.

"Confía en mi, por favor, señor
Déjame llevarla y traerle algo de comer."

"They are enclosures, the official said.
"We're uncomfortable with the term *'cage'*.
They are temporary structures of chain link."

A voice was heard in Ramah.
Rachel weeping for her children.

To comfort them, to warm them, to console them,
they have each been given a blanket
                                        made of foil.

At auction the Rubens sold
        for 75 million dollars.

And in the bramble a ram entangled:
O angel of outrage, where are you?

Rubens, Breughel, Poisson, Ghirlandaio.

Raytheon, Lockheed Martin/General Dynamics,
Northrup Grumman, General Electric.

Herod, Franco, Trump, Mohammed bin Salman.

Historians are skeptical the massacre took place.
Flavius Josephus does not mention it.

The Orthodox Church has for millennia held
that Herod, as punishment, was eaten alive by worms.

3. Sentinel

I show him,
now 3,
his birth

photo:

asleep,
fist
under his chin.

"No!" he says,
"Not me! *Not!"*

4. *Hold That Pose*

In old-time billowing shirtsleeves,
      baggy woolen pants,
           and ankle-high black cap-toes,
grandfather-like

      Edison, a picture of Edison,
as if he has just heard news
      from the prophets obviating hope
         of happiness,

of any, ever again...

      but no, his frown, his anger, his clean-
            shaven, cathode stare

is for his adversaries.

      Who owns the light?

A button, a toggle, a dimmer:
control and guidance
      systems: a satellite, its solar panels wings,
         a painting, hyper-realist, above
earth's marbled blue curve

figures a lovely emptiness, of grace,
(*artist's rendering* in fine print bottom right)
      better
much better than

a charred orb sulphured yellow
         as a smoker's fingers.

5. *Mundus et Infans*

From what region in the imagination
of celibate churchmen do they come,
these cherubs, wrists and ankles creased,
they are so plump, and much too heavy
for their tiny wings? Ideas, not children,
that have never matured, impossible,
equating helplessness with innocence,
wordless amnesia with paradise, so I
call bullshit on Paul: When I was a child,
I spake as a child, in pain, and asked
my questions clearly, in a sweeter voice
perhaps, but not less serious than now
when clarity remains at least as hard and
honesty much harder. I still play dead
to keep in practice since you never know.

6. *Tribute*

This man once,
he went down.

This time none,
not one man,
not one pill,
not one hope
could stop him.

Not one cry.

Not one hand
could reach him.

Not one lie
could save him.

He went down.

This man lived
where men fear
what they know

and knew what
he knew and
spoke the truth.

Not one bond
could turn him,
not one friend
could soothe him.

He went down.
We mourn him.

for Patrick McSorley

Note: Patrick McSorley was among the earliest and most powerful voices to speak out against the widespread sexual assault of children by Catholic priests. He had been assaulted as a 12 year old boy by Rev. John J. Geoghan, a notorious abuser with hundreds of victims. After a long struggle with addiction, likely a consequence of childhood sexual abuse, he died at age 29.

7. *Progress*

      Iphigenia

               Isaac

kids

      bugs

on the windshield ever since

story/explanation/lowdown/narrative/narration/citation/recital/report/take/
version/rundown/score/apologue/allegory/metaphor/myth/parable/fable/
discourse/propaganda/treatise/testament/epic/justification/rationale/excuse

            **WE'RE SORRY, SOMETHING WENT WRONG.
               PLEASE TRY YOUR QUERY AGAIN**

fish gotta swim
birds gotta fly
boats gotta sail

      fish, birds, boats,
               kids,
swim, fly, sail,

        die

      at the direction of frowning,
serious, disciplined men

         who grew up with me, in America,

on their bikes, on roller skates
      under the horse chestnut trees,

trading baseball cards they bought
        with money from their paper routes,

the nightmare true now, nightmare
                of my Cold War boyhood
        true
to children elsewhere.

And in the bramble a ram entangled
O angel of outrage, where are you?

Because everybody needs a job.
(We are one great mass of writhing flesh.)

Because fear begets profits and profits
        more nifty gadgets,

                first best gizmo off the line is always an idea,
an assumption,
        a mysterious, immaterial twin

to every sleek weapon thereafter,
                a prayer

to consecrate the idol. Years of this, generations,

        (Hey, I'm just trying to make a buck!)

O shake us, make our hearts
hammer shame-in-the-face.

Now blood drips from public monuments
like icicles in spring.

We no longer know how to know what we know.

                ERROR: 404: NOT FOUND

8. *In The Mean Time*

Between the launch and the blast
we drank to our prosperity.

The boys are off to prison or to war.
The girls carve crosses in their thighs.

Sirens, blue lights, shots fired.
Even enough is not enough.

The server's down. The safety's off.
History's a hoarder's burning house.

9. *Isaac's Dream*

Who's there? Who's there?
It's dark. I'm afraid. I can't see.
No one. Only an old nightmare.

Now I'm falling into nowhere
while a body looms above me:
who is it? Who's there?

Who's pulling my hair
and muttering so angrily?
No one. Only an old nightmare.

A hand on my throat: air!
I garble a choked plea.
Who's there? Who's there?

I hear moaning somewhere,
cry out, and wake abruptly.
No one. Only an old nightmare.

Slowly, I see the dream
was, in fact, a memory,
and I know who was there:
my father, my old nightmare.

10. *A Dainty Dish*

Sing a song of violence,
its pockets full of lies.

Four and twenty children
sent sailing off to die.

When the boat was sinking
the sharks began to sing.

Can we even let ourselves
imagine their suffering?

The keeper of the lighthouse
was counting out his money.

Politicians took to TV,
said the usual baloney.

The maid was in the garden
enraged by what she knows.

Along came Justice, smirking,
and thumbing its nose.

11. *Enfant Soldat*

"I used to be always shaking.
Some boys cried, but I was a shaking one.
The day of the trucks I wanted to run
but I was shaking and shaking. If I run?
Two boys who did was in the middle of the circle.
Never can I ever not be thinking of this now.
On the ground, boots on their backs
they are scared on their faces. And the boy who is beside me
they give him the gun. He was little,
one of those crying kind. Shoot them boys on the ground dead.
Shoot him and him dead, they say, him and him.
The crying boy he could not do it.
Never can I ever not be thinking of this now.
So the man, he was who drove the truck,
take back the gun and shoot him in his face.
Then he is right away dead. Quiet.
All around the circle then the man is walking, looking
in our faces and I cannot stop shaking.
When he make another boy the one,
make him to hold the gun, that boy
step to the boys on the ground and shoot their heads.
We all climb in the trucks then.
And that is how they took us to Mushasi camp. For training."

12. *Seer*

In Euripedes' dour version,
Artemis, to whom men pray
for permission to kill wild
creatures of her forests, spirits

Iphigenia away to Tauris
where she makes prophecy
of the single thing she knows,
denied by all who seek her:

children will be sacrificed
for advantage, for victory.
What she knows is always so.
It's almost too easy. Almost.

Hardest are the armored men
who clatter up her stairs.
She knows the harm they will do
and that no words will stop them.

Coda: *Uvalde, TX, 5/24/2022*

Another.

No not another, not
that cushion
of a word.

Yesterday
with my granddaughter, 3:

we lay on our bellies
on the warm pavement
watching ants.

Look look
that one's carrying something.

That his dead
brother he
bringing him home.

Acknowledgments

The author wishes to thank the editors of the following publications in which these poems first appeared, sometimes in earlier versions:

Betrayal: *Lily Poetry Review*
Horizon: *Pangyrus*
Wurst Haus: *The High Window (UK)*
D(r)one: *The Cincinnati Review*
Penitentiary: *The Manhattan Review*
Imagine a Future: *World Literature Today (under the title "In Which I Try to Imagine Justice.)*
Refrigerator: *The Harvard Review*
Contrast: *PN Review (UK)*
Shelter: *The Literary Review*
How to Get By: *World Literature Today*
They That Mourn: *Pensive: A Global Journal of Spirituality and the Arts*
Tenebrae: *The Baffler*
Last Hope: *The Woven Tale Press*
Kyrie: *PN Review (UK)*
Mt. Moriah: (published as "Climb") *Ibbetson Street*
How I Burned: *The Manhattan Review*
Bobber: *The Common*
Late Elegy: *Agni*
Trapdoor: *Salamander*
In Memoriam: *The Manhattan Review*
Solitude: *The Manhattan Review*
November Suite: *The Woven Tale Press*
Addict: *The Manhattan Review*
That Water: *The Literary Review*
Hurricane: *Agni*
Dusk: *The Manhattan Review*
Reflection: *The Manhattan Review*
O: *Agni*
Invocation: *Plume*
I Don't Recall Where We Were Going: *Lily Poetry Review*

A Summer Nap: *Poetry Northwest*
Solitude: *The Manhattan Review*
A Marriage: *The Hudson Review*
Happiness: *The Manhattan Review*
Remorse: *Agni*
A Love Song: *Pangyrus*
Raptor: *PN Review (UK)*
"Fantastic Voyage": *Lily Poetry Review*
Uvalde, TX, 5/24/2022: *Vox Populi*
Vaccine: *The Hudson Review*

A special thanks to my editor, Eileen Cleary. Thanks also to
Kathleen Aguero, Richard Cambridge, Dewitt Henry, Lee Hope,
Tom Mallouk, Michael Morse, Dennis Nurkse, J.D. Scrimgeour,
and Baron Wormser for their critical readings of several of
these poems.

About Richard Hoffman

Richard Hoffman has published four previous books of poetry: *Without Paradise; Gold Star Road,* winner of The Barrow Street Press Poetry Prize and the Sheila Motton Book Award from The New England Poetry Club; *Emblem*; and *Noon until Night,* which received the 2018 Massachusetts Book Award for Poetry. His other books include the celebrated memoirs *Half the House* and *Love & Fury,* the story collection *Interference and Other Stories,* and the essay collection *Remembering the Alchemists and Other Essays.* He is Emeritus Writer in Residence at Emerson College and Nonfiction Editor of *Solstice: A Magazine of Diverse Voices.*

www.ingramcontent.com/pod-product-compliance
Lightning Source LLC
Chambersburg PA
CBHW031446120626
46545CB00006B/2580